Communicate to Lead!

Influencing others for positive change...

Pastor Joel L. Rissinger, MA, MRE

4/5/2016

All rights reserved. No part of this publication may be reproduced or transmitted for commercial purposes, except for brief quotations in printed reviews, without written permission of the author.

Endorsements

"Communicate to Lead" will give you the insight into how communicating to connect will make you a better leader. It is a book that I will periodically review to refresh my communication skills.

Elliot Sirotnak General Manager, CoorsTek, Inc.; East Granby, CT

Every leader I know wants to share their passion with those around them. They want to connect in order to make a difference. The key to opening that door is to communicate. "Communicate to Lead" gives you the tools you need to communicate effectively in a way that makes a connection.

Deryk Richenburg, Senior Pastor, First Church of Christ in Wethersfield, CT

Communication is such an important & powerful facet of human life that at the Tower of Babel, God created various languages to separate the people, lest they do whatever they want! In his book, Pastor Joel walks us step by step through how we can communicate, unlike up to Babel, for the good & betterment of each other & society, once again Joel paints a clear picture as he has with his other writings, only this time on how important it is to lead & communicate in a strong & effective manner.

Al Stewart, D.D., Pastor, Forest Community Church, Forest, Virginia

Based on his training, experience, and desire to help leaders, Joel teaches about some of the most practical communication skills you'll ever need. Whether you're a pastor or executive; you'll find many helpful insights about how to be a better communicator and lead more effectively.

Dr. Brent Allen, District Executive Minister, Converge Northeast

Workshop with Newington Chamber of Commerce

Joel with John Maxwell

Teaching a "Speak to the Heart or, You'll Talk to the Hand" workshop

Karen Rissinger communicates to lead at a Mill Pond Church Event

To my wife Karen—You have influenced me for good since the day I met you. Your love for God, for me, for our family, and others has literally changed my life. Thank you!

To my son David—my prayer is that this book will serve as an inspiration to you long after I'm gone. Thank you for your love and you constant, helpful insights.

To my daughter Shelly & her husband Alex—You guys are what I want to be when I grow up. Thank you for your encouragement and for leading by example in all you do.

To Aadi, my sweet Granddaughter—By the time you can read this on your own, I trust you'll be a leader in your own right. May the principles in this book guide you always. I love you munchkin!

To the elders, leaders, and much-loved members of Mill Pond Church. You are the best spiritual family I could ever dream of or imagine. Thanks for the honor of being your pastor!

Forward

As a John Maxwell Team speaker, it's almost embarrassing to publish a book on leadership while in his impressive shadow. Nobody has written more on this subject than John and none as well. So, I'll preface this work by saying that my hope is to add value to the ultimate value-adder. That is, I believe this book to be supplemental by focusing more on communication as it relates to leadership. The idea for this book came to me while teaching one of our core Maxwell Group learning systems based on John's book, "Everyone Communicates, Few Connect." It seemed that some needed/wanted to go deeper into this aspect of what I call, "servant leadership communications." This book is my attempt to do so. My hope and prayer is that this will allow all who read it the opportunity to speak, write and teach in ways that truly lead to positive change in the lives of those they lead.

To that end,

Pastor Joel

Table of Contents

Chapter One: Just What Do You Mean, "Leadership?"......................p 11

Chapter Two: Communication is the Door, Connection is the Key...p 18

Chapter Three: Connecting with the Heart & Head............................p 29

Chapter Four: The Three Questions Everyone Asks..........................p 37

Chapter Five: Meeting the Three Basic Needs all People Share........p 51

Chapter Six: Assessing Personality and Motivation Without a Test..p 61

Chapter Seven: Listening--More Than "Half the Battle"....................p 88

Chapter Eight: Keynote Speaking vs. Toastmasters Training............p 101

Chapter Nine: Non-Verbal Communication & Learning Styles.........p 107

Chapter Ten: One-on-One Communication, the Crown Jewel.........p 116

Chapter Eleven: When to Use Email, Letters, & Text Messaging.....p 123

Chapter Twelve: Is Silence Golden? When Leaders Speak................p 130

Chapter Thirteen: How to Know Your Communication Worked.....p 133

Chapter Fourteen: Leadership Communication—Adding Value......p 138

Appendix:

* Footnotes..p 142
* About the Author...p 143
* Seminar & Keynote Speech Topics Offered...................................p 145
* The F.A.S.T. Track to Find and Equip New Leaders........................p 147
* The 4 Animal Profile Inventory..p 150
* Sample Feedback Form..p 151

Chapter One: Just What Do You Mean, "Leadership?"

For years, I believed that great leaders were born, not made. Sadly, I accepted my own leadership failings as just a lack of genetics. After all, some people just make it look so easy. And, even though I tried hard, it seemed some things were just impossible for me to accomplish.

Enter John Maxwell.

In his book, "21 Irrefutable Laws of Leadership," John defines leadership and then goes on to suggest that while certain in-born personality traits make a few of his laws easier to practice, all of the principles of good leadership can be learned and the habits lived-out REGARDLESS of personality, giftedness, etc.1

John's definition itself creates a broader, ever-widening relevance for the topic of leadership development. John simply says that leadership is "influence" and the purpose of good leadership is to add value to people around you. By this definition, everyone is a leader to one degree or another since we all influence people, hopefully for good.

This is not to cheapen or render meaningless the idea of positional authority, nor does it take away the challenge of influencing large groups of people in any setting. Rather, it just shows that we can learn to increase our influence (leadership) no matter what natural abilities we're born with.

For the purposes of this book, I'd like to add to John's definition. I'd like to suggest that true leadership IS influence, but that it's influence which produces noticeable or measurable change in those being led. I agree with the purpose John suggests because this should be positive change, thus adding value, but it has to be a real change. Otherwise, influence could be temporal or even imagined and thus of no real leadership value.

For example, it's said that people forget about 75% of what they hear within 48 hours. I remember visiting a small group meeting as a pastor years ago on a Thursday evening. At that time in my ministry, I used to preach and then give our group leaders a discussion outline based on the message so they could use it in their small group meetings each week. That particular week, the leader decided to have some fun by asking ME the first question. With a wry smile he turned to me in the meeting and said, "So Pastor, what was the MAIN lesson you gleaned from last week's sermon?"

I went completely blank.

Remember, I wrote the sermon, gave the sermon, wrote the outline, and was now sitting in a meeting just a few days later. Facing the first question in the outline, I had nothing but an old TV Screen test pattern in my head—white noise—that's it! I hadn't just forgotten 75%--I had lost 100%! What hit me was, if that's true for me—how much more so for the rest of the people in the room?!

If I had been relying on the content of that message to change the lives of the hearers—or even my own in this case—I'd be in for a rude awakening! There would be zero results. Did I influence them? Perhaps, subconsciously. But did I lead based on my new definition requiring some measurable change? Probably not!

So, before we go further, let me propose the following definition of true, positive leadership:

> *Leadership is influence which produces measurable, positive change in the lives of others. This can be developed or learned and is thus, intentionally contagious.*

I work with churches and small businesses primarily. Some of my clients are not people of faith and I'll ask that they bear with me for a moment because the last part of my definition reminds me of 2 Timothy 2:2 where Paul suggests that Timothy's leadership MUST pass on the truth to others who will in turn, pass it on to others...and so forth. Regardless of the topic, secular or sacred, I believe this is true. And it's true because leadership itself can be passed on as a skill.

But how?

I would be a fool at this point to try and reproduce what my mentor John Maxwell has done for 30 years. Nobody has done more to teach and enable leadership development than John. INC Magazine called him the number one leadership guru in the world.2 No living author has written and taught more on the subject—literally hundreds of millions of people have learned leadership from John. I suggest everyone take advantage of his over 70 books to develop leadership ability.

Having said this, one of John's books in particular has influenced me and is the launching pad for the ideas in this book. Several years ago, John wrote, "Everyone Communicates, Few Connect." To me, the idea of communicating to connect is where leadership development really begins.

If leadership is influence, it's important to recognize that communication is the primary method or key to influence. Still, as with my example above, if you don't connect when you communicate, that influence won't last and thus produce change.

This book is an attempt to help you make that connection so that true leadership, influence for measureable, positive change can occur. As with John's writings, please understand that you can learn it and pass it on. It's my prayer that you will!

Chapter Two: Communication is the Door, Connection is the Key

Some time ago, I wrote a blog entitled, "Leaders Who Communicate REALLY Lead." I'd like to share it with you here...

> *I've had an interesting career in that I've worked in the secular and sacred, the for-profit and not-for-profit worlds for many years. I've done consulting work, sales, chaplaincy, ministry, recruiting, marketing and more. When I'm introduced for a public speaking event, I often joke that my bio sounds like a guy who can't hold a job.*
>
> *But there's one thing I've seen consistently no matter where I go--leaders who communicate, lead well. And, those who don't...well, they just don't!*

Perhaps you've worked for the "strong, silent type" during your career. How was that? When it comes to leadership, silence isn't "golden." Typically, a lack of healthy and active communication leads to disaster.

That's not to say that all communication is good either. A boss who yells, insults, misdirects, complains, or wastes time with pointless diatribes in meetings is just as destructive as one who never shares or teaches. I would only clarify however, that negative communication isn't REAL communication anyway. It's just noise.

The key to leadership is communicating to connect. This is my "sweet spot" as a speaker, so I could talk about this for hours. In brief, leaders who can clearly communicate and connect with both the hearts and minds of those they lead will ALWAYS do better than others. People respond to this, productivity rises, morale improves, expenses and losses decrease--it's literally <u>all good</u>!

So how does one learn to lead via good communication?

I'd need hours to answer that fully, but here are some tips that anyone can implement to be a better leader, one who influences others and adds value to their lives...

> 1. You have to try. *I know this sounds silly, but you'd be amazed at how many people tell me, "Yeah, I know I don't really listen and I'm a bit blunt, but hey--that's just who I am!" If your attitude is that you communicate the way you communicate and nothing's going to change it, stop reading now. I can't help you. If you're OPEN to change...read on.*

2. You have to care. *One of the first questions people ask when they meet you or I is, "Do you care about me?" This may be a subconscious question, but make no mistake, they're asking it. Connecting with the heart means answering this and similar questions with a resounding "YES!" Still, you can't "fake it till you make it" when it comes to leadership communication. You either care...or you don't. People can "smell" hypocrisy a mile away under water. But, if you do care for those you lead...keep reading.*

3. Listen, listen, and then listen some more. When you're done, then listen. *The vast majority of communication issues I witness in business or even in people's private/social lives are based on a lack of solid listening skills. We teach some techniques in our workshops to assist with this and, in our coaching*

curriculum, we're focused on listening above all else. Still, there's really no magic here. You must actively and reflectively listen to communicate in a way that inspires others to follow.

4. Be transparent. *As I write today, Donald Trump is leading the polls in the republican primary race. To some, this is a mystery. I think it's plain and simple. People want to follow someone who shoots straight, says what he/she thinks, and someone who isn't afraid of what others may think when the speech is over. Whether you agree with Mr. Trump on policy issues or not, one thing is certain. He doesn't mince words, worry about being politically correct, or dance around issues when asked a pointed question. Leaders must be kind, but honest; direct, but sensitive; forthcoming, yet reflective in what they say or*

write. This isn't easy. Still, these are learned skills anyone can master and that's what I do-- I help leaders master these skills.

5. *Always add value. As mentioned above, many of us have had the "pleasure" of sitting through meetings that had no real purpose or value to us when doing our jobs. Nothing is more frustrating than being required to attend a meeting that doesn't help or inform you in a practical way. This is especially true when your desk is piled with unfinished projects. As a leader, it's important to ask yourself the following question re. every person you meet with either one-on-one or in a large group: "How will this meeting help _____ do his/her job better and/or grow as a person?" If you can't answer the question or if there's no good answer, don't bring that person to the meeting. It won't help--it will*

> *likely hurt your relationship and credibility with them. Even during informal conversation or the proverbial chat over the water cooler, leaders ALWAYS seek to add value.*

We will develop some of the ideas in this piece at length later in the book, but for now, we need to agree that if you can't communicate, you can't lead. It's the door—the opening, the first and primary step to true effective leadership. Unless through verbal and non-verbal means, people know what your vision, values, goals and/or objectives are; they will not and frankly CAN not follow you.

So leadership starts with communication for understanding, at least an understanding of how to begin to follow. Yet, as we discussed in chapter one, if there's no lasting connection, positive change won't occur. This is why I say that connection is the key to the door of communication. If you connect with people, you'll be able to communicate effectively for change. Conversely, if you don't connect, using my door analogy, you'll be locked-out.

Several years ago, my family and I were at a conference in Niagara Falls. We were seated near the front with a few thousand people behind us, when the speaker went on a rant saying, "We know the things I've been discussing are going to happen...but when, When, WHEN?"

Suddenly, our three year old daughter climbed onto her chair and before we could stop her, she put her little hands on her hips, and screamed, "I DON'T KNOW!"

She brought the house down...

We did the adult thing, we pointed to her, shrugged our shoulders and mouthed the words, "Someone else's kid!"

The point is, that even at age three, the speaker and my daughter had a connection. She understood him—she knew he was asking questions and that she didn't have the answer. There was a connection—but something else was missing...

This always reminds me of a preacher who was trying to make a point using all the tools he'd been taught in seminary. So using voice inflection while reading from the Bible, he shouted, "Be-Hold...I Come Quickly!" From the audience, he got crickets…no response. No "Amen," no applause, nothing, nada…zilch!

So, he'd been taught to gesture. He did. He read it again with wild movement. "Be—Hooold…I Come Quickly." Flat line…no response…nothing from his listeners!

So, in frustration, he backed up 15 steps, ran toward the podium, leaped into the air and yelled, "Be-hoooold I Come…" but he tripped on the podium, fell off the platform, and landed in the lap of a lady in the front row. Shoes, Bibles, papers, etc., went flying…people gasped…it was a disaster!"

Flabbergasted, he helped her up, dusted her off, helped her into her seat and said, "I'm so sorry Ma'am…I don't know how that happened." "It's OK Preacher," she said,

"I should have been ready for ya. You told me three times you was on your way!"

The preacher and the keynote speaker both made connections. One was mental, the other was physical, but neither had the complete picture. No, to make a true connection—to use the key to unlock the door to TRUE communication and thus EFFECTIVE leadership, one must connect with the mind—and most importantly, the heart!

So how does this happen? Read on my friend...read on....

Chapter Three: Connecting with the Heart & the Head

When I was 16, I "fell in love." Her name was Janet and her Daddy owned a pig farm, so naturally, I became a pig farmer too. I would go to her place after school and feed, slop, clean, and care for the hogs—for free. I was a big boy, so I used to carry two; 50 gallon milk cans full of water from the main barn to a poll barn in the back—just to show off.

Sadly, she never noticed.

Until one day. She walked up to me and asked me, "Hey why are you going the long way to the pole barn? You know it's a lot quicker to go straight out there!" She pointed across a long cesspool of pig slop—urine, mud, and of course—let me use a medical term--poo, that stood between the two buildings.

"Great idea!" I said and started to walk, and this time, she was watching. I lifted those milk cans high and began to "strut my macho stuff." Now what she knew, but I didn't know, was that in the middle of that pool of poo…there was a 6' deep and 7' wide hole. I was headed straight for it. I hit it "head on" and sank up to my forehead, filling my boots, pockets, everything with…poo!

Embarrassed and smelly, I walked home. Her mother must have called mine because Mom met me at the front door. "Unless you're naked," she said, "you've not coming in my house!" "But Mom," I protested, "I'm 16 years old! What if a car comes by?" "Naked or homeless," she said, "it's your choice. Lose the poopy clothes or stay outside!"

And that's how streaking was born…as Paul Harvey would say, "Young love + pig Doo-Doo = the birth of streaking. . And now you know…the REST of the Story!"

Now whenever I share this sad tale, people ask me, "Well…did you learn your lesson? Did you drop her? After all, she played you for a fool you know!?" And my answer?

OF COURSE NOT!

What's a little pig poo when you're "in love?" We actually never had a romantic connection, but we remain friends to this day (nearly 40 years later).

The point is, when you make what I call "a heart connection," people will literally swim through pig poo for you! Zig Ziglar put it this way. "Help people get what they want and they'll help you get what you want."[3] The heart connection—what people truly want at even a subconscious level—is the key to true influence and thus, true leadership!

The problem we have is that most of us were taught to make a mental connection, but we were likely never taught how to go deeper than that. Sales training, homiletics, apologetics, professional speaker's training, Toastmasters, you name it—most programs are designed to convince or explain, not often to convict or connect at an emotional or spiritual level. Yet it's at that subconscious, heart level that people make lasting decisions and true connections.

We see this in the political realm all the time. As I write this, we're in the midst of a presidential election cycle. Ugh! It's almost sickening to see how superficial and downright silly we've become. During the last two political elections, people admittedly voted based on a slogan. This time, they're voting based on who yells the loudest or who makes the wildest, most impossible-to-fulfill promises. Both parties are guilty, but since he won last time, let me use President Obama's first campaign as an example. People were polled by a couple of news outlets after the election and asked who they had voted for. Most said President Obama. When asked, "Why," most quoted his campaign slogan, "Hope and Change." When asked what they "hoped he (would) change," they were often speechless. They literally had no idea. They just liked the sound of his slogan. They knew little to nothing about him or his track record. They just liked "hope and change."

What people were literally saying in these interviews was that then-Senator Obama made them feel good. He connected with their hearts where other candidates did not. Agree with his policies or not, he made a heart connection—exclusively in many cases—and got elected as a result!

This is NOT to say that the mental connection doesn't matter—because it does. We must be organized in the way we present. We must use illustrations and interactive teaching techniques. We must do all the things we were taught to gain mental assent from those with whom we communicate. But Imagine what might happen if we consistently connected with their hearts—

their passion—and then led toward positive change. What might be possible if we add motivated application to understanding?

My point is that when we achieve the head and heart connection, who knows? People might go through "pig poo" for us too. Whether the path is easy or difficult, they'll follow us to incredible growth and transformation!

So just how do we make that heart connection?

Actually, the key to that connection is not based on us. It actually starts with our audience. Someone once said that what the audience wants us to know isn't more details about our product or service. It's not better presentation skills or a deeper understanding of the deep spiritual truths we hold so dear. No...what our audience wants us to know...is THEM. And to do that, we must consider the three most important questions on their minds when they meet or hear us for the first time. If we can answer these with a resounding, "YES!" we're connecting. If not, well...not so much. Let's explore these questions in some detail.

Chapter Four: The Three Questions Everyone Asks When They Meet You

John Maxwell says there are three questions people ask whenever they meet us or hear us speak for the first time:

1. Do you care about me?
2. Can I trust you?
3. Can you help me?

We'll look at each of these in some depth, but first let's consider how and why these questions are so important.

First, I don't want to suggest that these questions are asked consciously. In fact, most often they are subconscious, yet just as critical to the listener. We ask these because it's part of our reticular activating system—the system God designed in our brains to help us sort and filter information. If we were keenly aware and focused on all stimulus around us, we'd be overwhelmed, literally buried in sensory chaos. Instead, our minds allow us to focus on what matters most. Thus if someone cares for us, is trustworthy, and can add value to our lives—we pay them heed. Otherwise, forget it!

Never has this been more critical than in the 21st Century where our phones, the internet, TV, Radio, electronic billboards, and a hundred other sources fill our senses with information overload on a minute-by-minute basis. Listeners can only maintain sanity by sorting out what to listen to! Thus, these questions are vital to them—and to those of us doing the communicating. If these questions are answered with a resounding, "Yes," we're going to connect. If not, we will fail!

So how do we do that? Let's take each question separately:

Do You Care About Me?

In a world of narcissistic behavior and priorities, it's rare to find someone who really cares about anyone other than themselves. And, while there are techniques and approaches you can use to communicate care, I must start by saying that you cannot "fake it till you make it" on this question. People can "smell" hypocrisy a mile away!

The core of this question is critical. It is not "Do you care about my business," or, "Do you care about my wallet," or, "Do you care about my organization, church, program, etc?" The question is clearly, "Do YOU care about ME?" To get a "Yes" answer to this, you must demonstrate interest that goes beyond the surface. It starts with remembering names or, in the case of a large group, knowing some basics about their history, mission, etc. This, however is just the beginning.

One of my mentors, Steve Siebold, surveys his corporate audiences before giving a keynote speech or teaching a workshop. By the time he presents to them, he often knows more about their strengths, weaknesses, interests, and concerns then even their senior management. So when he speaks, he demonstrates concern and has the facts to back it up! One-on-one interaction is facilitated in this day and age due to the internet because through LinkedIn, Facebook, Twitter, and other programs we can learn a lot about people before we even meet them or talk at length.

One of my fellow-John Maxwell Team members saw this years ago during a meeting with Warren Buffett. After waiting 4 months for the appointment, she was told she only had 10 minutes. Rather than fire questions at him "rapid-fire," she did some research and found-out that his favorite beverage was Cherry Coke. So, before the appointment began, she said, "Mr. Buffett, I know we're short on time, but I thought you might like to start with a can of your favorite soft drink." She reached into her cooler bag, pulled out a can of coke, and put it on his desk. Mr. Buffett took the can, popped it open, took a sip, and said, "Young lady, you've got all the time you need." As I understand it, 90 minutes later, they finished their "10 minute interview."

What did she do? She demonstrated interest and care in Warren Buffett, not as an investment expert, but as a human being. Did it pay off? In spades!

Another way to communicate personal care is to understand personality and speak in ways specifically effective for that personality style. In my book, "Whole 4 Life," I talk a lot about personality. It's easier than you think to learn to assess the personality of individuals and groups such that you can choose to communicate with them in ways that are meaningful and effective. This also shows care and concern—even at a subconscious level.

For example, using the DISC profile, I like to refer to animal types to describe the four primary outstanding styles—the Lion, the Otter, the Labrador, and the Beaver (see profile quiz and descriptions in the appendix). Knowing which animal type someone reflects tells you a lot about how to connect with them. Lions, for example, like blunt and direct communication. Otters like to joke and laugh and appreciate a light-hearted approach. Labrador's don't like change or to feel rushed, so speaking slowly and emphasizing stability is key. Beavers like to follow the rules and do things right so having your facts together is paramount. Approaching each one appropriately says, "I care about YOU!"

Can I Trust You?

While it's true that trust takes time, there are some things you can do to accelerate the process. Surprisingly, one of these things is to be transparent and vulnerable. This is counter-culture to what most of us were taught, but nonetheless, it works.

Mitt Romney is a prime example. I know that the Romney campaign was repeatedly advised to "mess him up" prior to the election because he was seen as "a Ken doll" or "too perfect." They basically rejected this advice.

After the election the majority of those polled said that they believed Barak Obama could better identify with their life circumstances than could Mitt Romney. The impression that had was that he was too far removed from them and now-President Obama was not. I don't believe this to be true per se, but the lack of vulnerability hurt the Romney campaign—this is certain.

So go ahead and tell the personal stories. Use self-deprecating humor. Admit that you don't have all the answers. Thus, when you do share something about which you have conviction, you'll be heard!

My father, Warren Rissinger, was a great example of how to build and maintain trust. My Dad graduated from a tiny country school with 3 other people in his class. He had no college or trade school education, yet he knew how to quickly win people's trust with his humor, warmth and honesty.

I used to travel with my Dad in the summer when I had no school. He sold oil, paint, nuts and bolts to larger farms and highway departments. He'd talk to these guys about baseball, hunting, fishing, etc. and they loved him. One day, while we were standing in the shop talking to this farmer, he said, "Warren, I don't have time to check it myself so why don't you go take inventory, fill out an order and bring it back?" Dad did and the guy signed it without even looking. I was shocked!

In the car on our way to the next customer, I said, "Wow Dad! That guy was crazy. He didn't even look at what you wrote down. You could have sold him anything!" "That's right," Dad said, "one time! And that would have been the last time we ever did business. You see, he trusts me. He knows I'd never cheat him. That's why he'll do business with me for years Son and I value that trust more than money." Thus, a powerful lesson was etched on my 12-year-old brain!

Can You Help Me?

This is the question that makes sales people jump for joy and spring into action! "Why yes, I can help you with this… (Feature-function-benefit presentation ensues)." But that's not really what people are asking when this question is brought up. What they really mean is, "Will knowing and spending time with you make me a better person? Will you add value to my life?"

As a young man in my 20's I worked for a management consulting firm in NJ, Associated Business Consultants. The President, Mike Harkins, was an aggressive, driving leader. One day, he burst into my office and said, "I'll bet you that I can sell our service without ever discussing price, the competition, or anything else!"

"You're nuts," I replied, "How can you pull THAT off?" Mike continued to explain that to any prospect, (we did recruiting, but also sales training), the most important person in the room during any presentation was...HIM! Thus, by asking the right questions and listening well, you could close without doing a lot of talking.

I still wasn't convinced, so Mike challenged me to set-up an appointment with the CEO of a mid-sized company who had no knowledge of our services, our pricing (which was very unique), or how we compared to other recruiting firms, etc. I did set that appointment and Mike went on the call. Mike walked into the office, looked around, scratched his chin, and said, "Wow! This is impressive. I know we have business to discuss, but I'm curious—how did you end up in this position?" The CEO began to share his story and Mike continued to ask questions, questions that demonstrated an understanding of the criteria and motivating factors for each career move and major decision made. Mike was demonstrating, by listening and questioning, that he understood what it took to progress and succeed, as this man no-doubt had done.

After about an hour, the VP of Human Resources knocked at the door, peeked in, and said, "I'm sorry to interrupt boss, but we have that meting ...we need to go." The CEO looked at Mike, apologized, and then turned to the VP and said, "Listen, I just met this guy Mike. He's full of it, but I like him. I want you to give him a search assignment immediately and let's see how he does." He shook hands with Mike and left. Mike left with the contract and it did get signed. He had closed a sale without ONE mention of our unique approach, our pricing, or anything else for that matter. What he HAD done was show that he understood what it took to win...and that was enough.

The key is that Mike demonstrated his competence, not by speaking, but by listening. Reflective listening, becoming a verbal mirror by repeating what the speaker has said in your own words until he/she agrees that you've understood, is the key here. It's also a matter of asking the right questions. John Maxwell's book, "Great Leaders ask Good Questions," is a must have resource on this topic.4

But the real foundation of this kind of listening and questioning comes from wanting to add value to people and from understanding the basic needs every human being has. If you truly desire this, then it's important to "go deeper" into the basic psychological need of those you lead and communicate with.

John Maxwell also likes to say that there are three of these primary needs shared by all of us. Understanding them allows us to answer question three, "Can you help," with a resounding, "YES!" Frankly, meeting these needs helps us connect by answering all three of the questions we've been discussing. We'll look at those need in our next chapter.

Chapter Five: The Three Basic Human Needs all People Share

The three primary needs of all human beings are to believe, to belong and to become. We must believe in something greater than ourselves, belong to an organization bigger than ourselves, and see that we're becoming someone better than ourselves, today. If we help people meet these needs, they will connect with us and grow in powerful ways.

Believe

I love the story of the outspoken Christian woman who used to pray aloud on her front steps every day, thus driving her atheist neighbor crazy. They had argued over this, but nothing had really changed. One day, she walked outside, looked heavenward and shouted, "Lord!

I know you'll provide 'cause you always do, but I'm out of food and I'm hungry. Please Jesus, make a way!"

"Now I've got her," her neighbor thought, "I'll prove there is no God!" So he ran to the supermarket, bought two bags of groceries, raced back to her house, placed them on the steps, rang the doorbell, and hid in the bushes nearby. Soon, the woman came out to check the mail and saw the groceries by the door. Without hesitation, she looked up and shouted, "Thank you Lord! I knew you'd come-through." "A-HAH!" the man shouted as he leaped from the bushes, "Now I've got you! There is no God. I brought those groceries, not your God!" Without missing a beat, the woman bowed her head and prayed, "And Lord, not only did you provide for me as promised, but you made the Devil himself pay the bill. Thank you Jesus!"

Whether or not you're a person of faith, it's a fact that we all come with a built-in need to worship and trust in something other than ourselves. The Bible says God made us that way by placing "eternity in (our) hearts (Eccl. 3:11)." If you doubt that belief is a basic need, go to a Buffalo Bills home game in January. You'll see people half naked, painted blue and red, screaming and jumping up and down in sub-zero temperatures. Now if that's not worship, I don't know what is!

No matter what you offer when you speak, you must show the listener that you're providing a chance to believe and trust in something greater. A greater principle, purpose, plan, or practice that will lead to a fulfillment of the other needs below. You can do this with words, but you must also be living it such that it's clear that you believe yourself and want to share it.

Belong

I speak at a lot of Rotary clubs and I am a Rotarian myself. In fact, I'm an officer and board member in my local club. I mention this because I see Rotary offering business people, young and old, a chance to belong to something greater—an organization doing great works around the world that none of us could accomplish alone. Sadly, many local clubs have done a poor job communicating this to the younger generation—those under 35 and are thus shrinking in size.

When you speak, network, blog or interact, you must show that you belong to something greater and so can your listeners. Most social media marketing companies get this and want you to "Like" their page and become part of a community, not just buy a product and "move on." If people understand that they become part of something by working with you, you will automatically be adding value and answering the third primary question (Can you help me?) with a, "Yes!"

Become

Of the three basics, this is most important. Since we're defining leadership as influence for the purpose of creating measurable, positive change; helping people become better is fundamental. If I help people improve/grow, my leadership influence grows. Thus, my opportunity for success and significance increases dramatically.

So how does this happen?

John's book, "Becoming a Person of Influence," is extremely helpful here, but let me summarize with a few principles.5 In essence, we help people become greater when we:

- Encourage—We say things that lift them up. An old pastor friend of mine used to love to say, "Encouragement must be encouraging, to the one needing encouragement." Thus, there's an individuality to this in that we must know the person well enough to understand what to say/do in order to lift their spirits and truly help them.

- Challenge—This is harder in that there's a fine line between challenging someone and pushing them or making them feel discouraged. Still, to believe that they are capable of more is a priceless benefit.

- Inspire—Inspiration is also somewhat personal in that sources of inspiration aren't always universal. Still, the key is to move the person to believe that they are capable of more and that it's OK to dream. We live in a world that kills dreams. Inspiration moves us to revive and enhance them.

- Teach—Knowledge is power, so passing it on will always have the potential of improving the hearers. Still, remember that with teaching there are three rules, just like the proverbial "3 rules of Real Estate." The "3 Rules of Real Estate" are "location, location, and location." Likewise, the 3 rules of Teaching are "application, application, and application." Therefore, when you teach, you MUST show how to use what's being taught or it will likely be forgotten. If it's forgotten, there will be no value added.

- Mentor—A good mentor takes what is taught and demonstrates application. The most common model is, "I'll tell you, I'll show you, I'll watch you, I'll help you adjust, and then I'll send you on your own." Of course, good mentors remain available for years to answer questions, clarify applications, etc.

- Coach—Within the context of the John Maxwell Group and the teaching of leaders like Christian Simpson, (see www.johnmaxwellgroup.com), coaching is not instructive nor is it directive. A good coach asks questions and listens well to help his clients understand themselves. The goal is to learn to help people understand the truth within their subconscious mind and also to see and reject the lies they may have believed.

As stated above, a number of these things are personal and individual. So, in our next chapter, we'll talk about how to assess personality and use the understanding of personality to connect and lead/influence others for good.

First, let's review. We've seen that leadership is adding value with measurable, positive change. We've considered communication as the door to good leadership and connection is the key to opening that door. We've talked about the importance of connecting with both the hearts and minds of those we lead. We've also seen how the heart connection occurs through answering some critical questions and meeting basic human needs.

Now, we'll go even deeper. Because human beings are so unique, we have to understand them more individually and specifically to effectively communicate to lead. Thus, we'll look at motivation and personality to "fine tune" our ability to reach them individually or in large groups.

In the last half of the book, we'll look at techniques. We'll consider ways to build our listening skills, public speaking abilities, the use of non-verbal techniques, written communication and more.

But first, let's take a closer look "under the hood." Let's consider personality and motivation and how to measure it effectively when sharing with and leading others.

Chapter Six: Assessing Personality & Motivation & Using it to Connect

When I started my career right after college, I was hired to recruit and interview candidates for Associated Business Consultants, a management consulting firm serving clients like Johnson & Johnson, Eastman Kodak, and others. My first assignment was to become proficient at the use of the DISC profile, a popular personality assessment tool. I did. In fact, I became so comfortable with DISC, I could meet someone, talk for a few minutes, sketch their profile on a napkin, give them the inventory, score it, and find that about 80% of the time, my guess sketch on the napkin was almost identical to the actual scored results.

Later, I connected with Dr. Mels Carbonnel, the founder of Uniquely You, a company focused on personality and spiritual gift assessment (www.uniquelyyou.com). Mels trained and certified me as a behavioral specialist and co-authored my book, "Whole 4 Life," along with Dr. Glenn Sunshine. The detailed description Mels gives of the DISC profile in the book is powerful and extremely helpful in understanding personality and style.6

I give you this background to present the dilemma I faced after all this experience. I knew how helpful personality profiling could be, but I also knew that most people couldn't give people an inventory or "test" when first meeting them on a date, making a sales call, or giving a speech to hundreds at a time. So the question was, how could the DISC methodology be taught and used without administering paperwork or a computer-based inventory?

That's when I remembered my experience sketching people's style on cocktail napkins. If I could learn to do that, anyone could—or at least they could learn to measure and assess the outstanding characteristics without a written inventory. Since that time, I've been teaching people that very skill as a primer for good communication.

In my workshops, we start by describing the four outstanding characteristics of D.I.S. & C. using animals: The Lion, Otter, Labrador Retriever, and the Beaver. The first goal is for participants to determine which one represents them. Then, based on that understanding, we teach them some techniques of assessing others based on communication. Of course, the information in my book goes deeper, but still, we can do basic assessments quickly using my methodology and then communicate in more meaningful ways based on that.

Let's look at each of the four animals, determine our own style, and then talk about how to assess others. We'll close this chapter with a brief conversation on how to communicate with each one.

The Lion

As you might guess, lions are the "Kings of the Jungle." They're bold, loud, decisive leaders. They get things done. They drive for results. However, since every strength has a corresponding weakness, they may also leave a wake of bodies—people who were "run over" in the process. Lions may not even be aware of the fact that this had happened. They can be blunt and not even know how it affects people.

I worked for a lion once who used to bring people to tears in staff meetings. Just as lions are direct, they appreciate others being direct with them. In fact, they may not even hear a subtle approach. So, I walked up to him and said, "Hey! You need to knock it off or you're going to lose people!" "What?" he replied, "What do you mean?" I explained it and offered to stand at the back of the room during the next meeting and make a choking gesture if he started down an offensive path. He agreed. This simple change saved stress and probably prevented a couple of unnecessary resignations.

On the positive side, lions are great leaders and will accomplish great things. If you're a lion, you like the facts, the bottom line and find a lot of extra talk "frustrating." You like to be in charge and appreciate finding ways to get things done.

The Otter

Otters are the "life of the party." If you've ever watched an otter in the zoo or in the wild, they literally play. Scientists find it frustrating to "peg" the behavior of an otter as a survival, mating, hunting, or other activity. Frankly, Otters like to have a good time and can do so even if they're alone.

Human "otters" aren't much different. They are the one telling jokes and making everyone feel welcome and happy. They are great with people, but sometimes not so great with details, reports, administration, etc. They are influencers, not accountants or engineers. They make great sales people, but need an administrative assistant to do the paperwork or they may end-up being fired.

If you're an otter, you like stories and just being with people. You don't like being in a cubicle or office by yourself. If you're talking with an otter, don't just cut to the "bottom line." He/she will like hearing a few jokes first. On the other hand, don't expect a lot of spreadsheets or data analysis from an otter…it just "ain't happening."

<u>*The Labrador*</u>

My dog Koda is part lab. My favorite times with him are sitting by the fireplace with him by my side. Just sitting with him, scratching behind his ears and watching the fire relaxes me. I'm the poster child for ADHD ("Look—Squirrel!"). Koda instinctively likes to calm me with his very presence. That is a CLASSIC lab trait.

Labs like stability and will fight to create it. They maintain systems well, but hate change. The antithesis of my personality, labs are phlegmatic and hate being around hyperactive people too much.

If you're a lab, you will gravitate to or create stability wherever possible. You want people to speak slowly and softly to you. You want to maintain the status quo and have little tolerance for people who generate a lot of changes in life or business. You're OK with maintaining systems, but really dislike trying new ones which may or may not have been fully tested.

The Beaver

As you may have noticed in the wild, beavers are very industrious. I grew-up hunting, fishing, and trapping on a regular basis. Often, when we'd encounter a beaver dam, we'd kick a hole in it and then stop back the next day to see what had happened overnight. Usually, not only was the hole repaired, the dam was fortified and stronger than it was the day before.

Beavers are good with numbers and details. They follow the rules and know the rules well. They make great accountants, engineers, architects, etc. The problem with beavers is that they WILL follow rules, even if the rules are in need of changing/disregarding. You'll never see a beaver drive the wrong way down a one-way street, even if there's no other way out and the entire neighborhood is on fire.

Beavers do great work and are accurate. The other problem they run into is when there's a deadline, they will struggle between honoring the deadline "rule," and getting the job done "right." They are perfectionists and feel torn or frustrated in these circumstances.

If you're a beaver, you like details and lots of facts. You like to consider all the options before making a decision and hate feeling rushed. Whereas the lion wants the bottom line, the otter wants to know how much fun it will be, and the lab wants to see how things will be "smooth" or "stable," beavers want the number and the details. Without this, they feel very uncomfortable and may get angry.

So which of these four best describes your personality?

Now before you say it, let me affirm that EVERYONE is a combination of these four. In fact, my studies suggest that there are 30 classic types or combinations and almost an infinite number of subsets under those 30. Still, every one of us has one of these four that stands out overall. To pick yours, ask yourself this question,

"Under pressure, am I more lion-like, otter-like, lab-like, or beaver-like?" The answer to that question give you your baseline or primary characteristic.

In other words, if under pressure you push to get things done and blow through the problem, you're a lion. If, on the other hand, you find yourself joking around or escaping to hang-out with and have fun with friends, you're an otter. If pressure leads you to try to slow everything down and create a softer, more stable environment, you're a lab. Finally, if pressure leads you to double-check your figures or do more research, you're probably a beaver. We've included a simple animal-formula profile inventory in the appendix to help you narrow this down.

So how can you assess and then communicate with each of these personality types?

First, remember to beware of what I call "personality-projection." We tend to project on others what we have in ourselves. If I'm a lion, I'll see lions everywhere and interpret most behaviors as lion-like behaviors. The truth is however, they may not be at all. Try to be objective. Here are some questions to ask as you meet and talk with people:

1. Does this person seem more interested in facts or feelings?
2. Does this person seem to want to have fun more than get things done?
3. Is this person a risk taker or do they seem to seek security/safety?
4. Does this person like details or are they bottom-line-oriented?
5. If I asked them, would they likely say they are a lion, otter, lab, or beaver?

Frankly, you CAN ask and people often enjoy talking about themselves in these terms. Some of my most enjoyable workshops over the years involve self-discovery using the animal or the pure DISC inventories with discussion. Nothing precludes you from doing the same one-on-one.

Once you have a pretty good handle on who and what you're dealing with, here are some great communication tips. I'll refer you to my book, "Whole 4 Life" and Dr. Mel's website, www.uniquelyyou.com for more information.

- LIONS—Be brief, be direct, cut-to-the-chase, be decisive, and show the bottom-line results or point you're making as soon as possible. Ask the lion about his/her conquests and success.

Find out what he's trying to achieve and quickly point-out how you'd be able to help.

- OTTERS—Smile, have fun, tell jokes, tell stories, and weave your message into something entertaining. Get the otter to talk about his/her last vacation or some funny story/joke he's heard recently. Show him/her how your topic or product will make life more enjoyable.

- LABS—Speak softly and slowly. Don't rush, look away, or seem distracted. Don't talk about how busy you are. Ask the lab to describe something he/she's done for ages and how it is reliable, dependable, and foundational. Show how what you're discussing creates stability and long-term reliability.

- BEAVERS—Similar to the LAB. Remember that most Beavers are almost labs but value hard work and accuracy. Use data, facts, figures, spreadsheets and historical proof when talking to beavers. Don't joke around too much and don't put-down the rules. Show how your solution will help the beaver get more done, more accurately, within the rules. Get him/her talking about their most perfect project or most successful program.

There are no guarantees with communication, but these tips can go a long way toward avoiding misunderstanding and thus influencing for good. If you'd like more information, try attending or purchasing a recording of or seminar, "Speak to the Heart...or, You'll Talk to the Hand." It contains some "food for thought" which you might find helpful on this topic.

Motivation

I've mentioned the book already, but I know of no better way to address this subject than to take an excerpt from my book, "Whole 4 Life:"

Passion. It's a word we throw around frequently in our culture. We understand that romance is fueled by passion and that it's fun and exciting. We understand that business thrives when leaders and customers are passionate about a product or service. We believe that life in general is more enjoyable when we have passion.

But how do we find our motivation and fuel our passion so that we can see these results and experience that joy?

Part of the answer starts with another question: What do you love? Assuming no financial or arbitrary limitations and imagining for a moment that you "couldn't fail," what would you do with your life? What kind of job would you have? Where would you live? Who would you spend time with?

Answering these questions can help you understand your passion and thus direct your life toward things that feed it.

We believe that the passion discovery process starts with understanding our purpose for being here. If I realize that I was created for a purpose, I can seek a sense of calling from the Creator. On the other hand, if I reject the notion of Intelligent Design, I'm left to pursue passion based on an internal sense of motivation.

As a pastor, I will meet and interact with many people who are spiritually seeking God. They normally believe that God exists as a first cause/Creator of the universe, yet they are not sure beyond that. At the behest and encouragement of my friend Gary Rohrmeyer, I have learned to ask them, "Do you believe everyone is on a spiritual journey?" Even atheists will normally say, "Yes." Then I ask them, "So where are you on your journey?"

They normally stare at me like the proverbial "deer in the headlights."

Gary's "Spiritual Journey Guide" has become a powerful component in our ability to assess people's spiritual health because it gives people a visual way to answer the question about their stage of spiritual development. Knowing this is a starting point from which we offer multiple growth and discovery options. Many churches already have these options in place, for instance, Rick Warren's 101-401 Discipleship Diamond. For others, we work with you to suggest alternatives.

Next, since the need to understand motivation is important as a second step for those who know their created purpose and a first step for those who choose not to discover this spiritual foundation, we will start with this element for the purpose of this chapter. How do we identify our primary motivation and what do we do to feed it once it is discovered?

Abraham Maslow postulated that our motives move up and down based on certain human needs. At the bottom of what is often called his pyramid or hierarchy of needs were basic needs: food, clothing, and shelter. One step up from that is security or safety needs, where we know that our lives and basic provisions are not in jeopardy. Once these two levels of need were met, Maslow believed, we could move up the hierarchy three more levels—affiliation, achievement, and finally, self-actualization.

According to Maslow, people continue to progress up the pyramid such that after one level of need is met, they then move forward. However, if one of the lower level needs fails, Maslow suggested that we would regress to that level and be motivated by that need until it was met. While we believe Maslow was right when it comes to basic or security needs, we disagree with regard to the three top tiers. We believe that most people "lock-in" or stabilize on one of those levels for most, if not all of their adult life. Even if a lower level need arises, it is our experience that people will pursue it, and fill it, without losing what we call "primary motive."

It is our conviction that there are three primary motives: Affiliation, Achievement, and Influence. Once you discover which of these primary motives are in place in your life, you can begin to make better choices for relationships, business, service, and life. To help you in that process, let's discuss each one briefly. Our motivational assessment tool can be useful in this discovery, as would a consultation with one of our associates.

Affiliation

The need for affiliation is present in all human beings. The famous song, "No Man Is an Island," illustrates this well. We all need social contact. Still, we need to differentiate between this common human need and the primary motive of affiliation.

The key question is this: What inspires you and gives you the energy to do something? If the answer centers around other people or just being with a group of people, you may be an affiliation-motivated person. A truly affiliation motivated individual could be happy doing virtually any job or service if they felt a close connection with a team or group of people also doing that job or being in that environment. It's not money, challenge, influence, a good benefit package that motivates the affiliation-motivated person, it's the relationships he/she has at work.

Great job settings for affiliation-motivated people include customer service groups, secretarial pools, and in some settings, project teams—assuming that deadlines and performance measurements are flexible.

Achievement

Achievement is measurable accomplishment and achievement-motivated people like to measure themselves against others or against high standards. These folks like other people and have social needs like anyone else, but they will work and be happy only in places where they feel challenged and can measure their progress. Further, they will even be content working alone and may work for little cash—as long as they feel they're doing something unique and record-worthy.

An achievement-motivated person needs measurement and competition. Certain government positions or repetitive, production positions would literally drive them crazy. Good jobs for achievement-motivated people include jobs with a P&L accountability, sales, or construction/trade jobs where on time completion is critical.

Influence

Influencers are power-people. This doesn't mean they are "controlling" in a negative sense. It does mean that they must work with people and feel that they have influence. They are often referred to as rich or "money-motivated," but money is only a means to an end for them. If they believe that having money and purchasing fine-quality goods will give them more influence, they will do so. They may not even like boating, for instance, but if having a yacht gives them a means to have impact with a certain group of people, they'll buy one.

Influencers need to lead. This may or may not involve a title, but they need to feel and experience the impact of their influence on others. Good jobs for influence-motivated people include executive management, sales/marketing, finance, and small business ownership.

Which are you?

Here are some questions that will help you identify your primary motivation:

1. *What was your favorite job and why was it your favorite?*
2. *What is your favorite hobby and why?*
3. *Who are your closest friends? What do you think are their primary motivators?*
4. *What is your net worth? If you don't know, you can rule out "Influence."*
5. *Do you post trophies, awards, or other certificates of achievement in your home and office?*
6. *Do you run on a daily "to do" list? How do you feel when you check off an item on that list?*

7. When you get excited about a project or an activity which is the most important/common factor:

   a. The people involved?

   b. The challenge or potential uniqueness involved?

   c. The fact that this activity/project will give you an "in" to make a difference in the lives of others or the success of your organization?

If you've answered these questions and you still are unsure of your primary motive, please feel free to contact our office for a consultation. You can reach us at our primary email address, joelrissinger@communicatetolead.com.

Once you've discovered your primary motive, the next step is to look at how this impacts your relationships. In brief, you will likely find that you are drawn to and thus closest to people who are motivated by the things that inspire and motivate you. Still, there are exceptions to this rule normally having to do with personality, spiritual giftedness, etc. We discuss more of this under "Person" and in our DISC profile materials.

How do you deal with people whose primary motivations differ from yours? Which motivational styles will you feel most comfortable with? What about dating and romantic relationships/marriage? Do you understand how you interact and can best connect with the opposite sex?

For married couples or for couples dating exclusively, we use the Prepare-Enrich relationship inventory (www.prepare-enrich.com). Just as with our other tools, Prepare-Enrich does two things:

1. Assess the current state of a couple's relationship.

2. Provide tools to leverage strengths and improve growth areas/weaknesses.

For pastors, counselors, and mentor couples, we recommend a one day certification workshop to license them to use Prepare-Enrich to assist couples in this journey. This *powerful tool has been used by over 2.5 million couples worldwide. I have found it helpful in my 25 year ministry for both premarital counseling as well as with married couples in conflict. You can learn more at www.prepare-enrich.com.*

In any leadership scenario, the benefits of knowing your passion and understanding the passion and heart of others are virtually limitless. You can connect with the heart, not just the head when you understand passion. And, once you've connected with the heart, people will follow you through thick and thin!7

Summary

Knowing someone's personality type and primary source of passion/motivation give you an advantage. It's an advantage not to manipulate, but to communicate. It's an opportunity to connect based on what matters most and to use the best methodology to share. Why? So you can lead, that is, influence to add value resulting in positive, lasting change.

However, none of this can happen without the subject of our next chapter, effective listening. We've seen why connecting with the heart and the mind is critical. We've looked at some practical ways to do it inclusive of truly understanding the other person's motivation, personality, etc. Now let's look at the most powerful connection tool we have: effective listening!

Chapter Seven: Listening--More Than "Half the Battle"

I once had a couple argue in front of me for 45 minutes. "Why did you let it go on that long?" you may ask. Well, for the first 20 minutes, it sounded like they agreed but they were still arguing. "I must be missing something" I thought, "It sounds like they agree." After 20 minutes, I was convinced that I wasn't missing anything—<u>they</u> were!

So, I let it go on several more minutes thinking, "They're going to see it…they have to! When they didn't, I yelled, "TIME OUT!" I turned to her and said, "Do you believe A, B &C." She said, "Yes." I said, then "Shhhh." I turned to him and asked the same question and he said, "Yes I do." "So," I concluded, "you're 100% in agreement, but you're still arguing. In what parallel universe does that make sense because it sure doesn't make sense in this one does it?"

The problem wasn't that they couldn't speak. They were both quite open and eloquent. No, the problem was that they weren't listening. Yet, had you asked them, they both would have claimed they were listening and getting the clear message from their partner.

In brief, the problem this couple had, and frankly, the problem most human beings have with listening is in a word, FOCUS! We're focused on the wrong things when we communicate and thus we "miss one other." Essentially, we focus on what we're going to say and thus miss what the other person is actually saying. Lack of focus on the speaker is the problem. Therefore, renewed focus is the cure.

The Epistle of James puts it this way, "Let every one of you be swift to hear, slow to speak, and slow to wrath (James 1:19)." I've always maintained that IF someone is swift to hear, he will therefore be slow to speak and then slow to become angry, partially because there will be fewer misunderstandings.

Dr. Stephen Covey in his book, "7 Habits of Highly Effective People," says that we should "Seek first to understand...then, to be understood." I would argue that this is more than half the communication "battle." 8

The best way to fix this is the use of I language and reflective listening. To address this, let me quote from my book, "The Crucified Couple:"

"When my wife and I do couples counseling, we use two tools popularized by Life Innovations, Inc. and their Prepare-Enrich program. The first tool is assertiveness using what I call, "I-language." I'll come back to this. The second tool is the use of reflective listening. Of the two, this is the hardest to learn and yet is the more powerful communication device I've ever witnessed.

When reflectively listening, a person repeats back what they've heard their partner say, using their own words, until their partner says, "That's it! You've understood me." Then—and ONLY then—the listener is allowed to express his/her own view and the roles reverse. The goal for the listener is not to necessarily agree, but to clearly and completely understand what their partner is saying. In fact, they may totally disagree with what's being said, but can still demonstrate that they've heard. Sometimes, they get to "hear" what their partner is NOT saying.

Sometimes, they don't just understand their partner...they help their partner understand themselves!

Larry and Kellie

A few years ago, I was doing premarital counseling with a beautiful young couple. I'll call them Larry and Kellie. Larry was a pastor's son—young, handsome, smart, and likeable. Kellie was a beautiful musician, newly graduated from college and working for a small church as a choir director and keyboard player. When I asked them to practice the use of "I language" and "Reflective Listening," a miraculous thing happened...and I got to witness it.

Before I describe the scene in more detail, let me quickly define "I language." "I language" is an assertiveness tool where the speaker uses the word "I" more than "you." So for example, if I want my wife to pick up her mail left lying around the house, I might normally say, "You need to pick us your mess. You always leave junk lying around. You're driving me crazy!" That would likely result in an argument or the silent treatment (fight or flight) as a response. As an alternative, I can use "I language" by saying, "Honey, I have a problem. I get very agitated and I feel stressed when there's a lot of clutter. I would feel more at peace if you could try to keep your mail in one place or toss it if you don't want it. I want to be less stressed toward you. I don't want the clutter to be a conflict because I love you."

With "I language," I'm saying the same thing, but "owning" the issue and framing it in a way that's less threatening to my spouse.

OK, now back to Larry and Kellie. As an exercise, I asked them individually to write down three things they'd like more or less of in their relationship and how they'd each feel if these things came to pass. I told them not to share them with their partner yet, just to write them down so we could share them using "I language" and "Reflective Listening."

When it came time to share, Kellie went first. She looked into Larry's eyes and said, "I wish we could be more spontaneous." Larry looked at me. I quickly directed him to look at her and reflect. He said, "So...you want us to be more 'off the cuff...right?" "Yeah..." she said hesitantly. Then they both stared at me as if they'd just pretended to listen to a four hour lecture in ancient Gaelic.

I looked at Kellie and said, "That's not all you're looking for—is it?" "No" she replied. So I looked at Larry and told him to ask her a question. "Can you give me an example?" "Sure," she said. "Remember that time we were driving and saw that carnival on the side of the road. We stopped and ended up spending the day. We had cotton candy and rode rides. We laughed and laughed. It was awesome!" "So," Larry stuttered, "You want us to do things that aren't planned...right?" "Yeah..." she said sheepishly.

It was at that moment that I realized something important. The beautiful thing is, Larry recognized it also. Kellie didn't know how to express what she wanted. She wasn't even clear on it herself—she just instinctively knew that something was missing. Instantly, Larry was "all over it." "OK, OK," he started, "So tell me this—besides the fact that it wasn't planned, what WAS it about that day that made it so special?" "Oh...that's a great question," Kellie said, "I think it was that we didn't talk on our phones, we didn't have to rush, we never looked at our watches, our conversations weren't interrupted...." "Wait!" Larry exclaimed, "I think I've got it! What made that day so perfect was that it was focused time. I focused on you. You focused on me. We weren't *distracted by all the projects and people and schedules we're always slaves to. What I think you want is more focused time for our relationship. That's what I want too. I love you!"*

Kelly stood up and with tears in her eyes; she hugged Larry like he had just returned from a tour of duty in Iraq. I felt like it was a holy moment and I should sneak out of the room to leave the two of them alone. It was beautiful! Why? Because, not only had Larry used reflective listening to hear his sweetheart's words, he had heard her heart. Not only did he hear what she said, he heard what she didn't say. Not only did he make sure he understood her—he helped her understand herself! And that my friends, is miraculous.

Now let's suppose Larry thought Kellie's desire or idea here was ridiculous. Let's say he felt that they had plenty of time alone and plenty of focused relationship time away from family and friends and schedules, etc. Let's say Larry was frankly sick and tired of spending one-on-one time and really missed spending time with all of their friends. Let's say, Larry felt pressed to share this with Kellie because his social butterfly need was dying on the proverbial branch!

The fact that he had heard Kellie and helped her understand her own need would go a long way in helping her be open to him sharing an opposing view, would it not? Further, if Larry was willing to sacrifice some of this to help Kellie feel more loved, do you suppose Kellie's desire would be do sacrifice as well? What would be the likelihood of Kellie compromising by giving a few more hours of social crowd time if Larry had understood her heart, validated it, and FIRST given her more alone time by his own free will choice?"9

While this is a couples example, the practical use of "I language" and "reflective listening" can go a long way toward improving our ability to listen well and truly understand one another. There are other listening techniques which can help with large audiences as well. As I mentioned earlier, professional speaker Steve Siebold surveys his audiences in advance whenever possible to understand them and help make his content more relevant to their needs. The use of the internet and all its wonders allows us to "know" those we're trying to communicate with far better than our ancestors could have known any audience they addressed—large or small.

The question is, "do we?" Do we take advantage of these things or do we assume things or ignore others altogether as we spew forth our ideas?

I'd be remiss if I closed this chapter without discussing the use of questions. John Maxwell wrote an excellent book entitled, "Good Leaders Ask Great Questions." 10 highly recommend it. In order to listen well, you have to have something to hear. In other words, if your audience isn't speaking to you, you can't hear and comprehend. Questions solve this problem. Great questions lead to tremendous benefits:

( ) You'll hear and understand more from the answers you receive.

( ) You'll demonstrate care and compassion by what you ask and how you ask it.

( ) You'll demonstrate competency since your knowledge and ability will shine through the questions you ask.

Etc...

In other words, learn to ask great questions and you'll enhance your ability to listen and thus communicate to lead.

Chapter Eight: Keynote Speaking Versus Toastmaster's Training

There are two things I need to clarify before I go too far in writing this chapter:

- First, I've technically never been in a Toastmaster's Club or even a meeting. I WAS a very active member of Spokesman Club, a spin-off of Toastmaster's for close to 10 years however, and found the experience very rewarding.

- Second, I thus have nothing bad to say about Toastmaster's Clubs. I think they serve a wonderful purpose in teaching people how to overcome the fear of public speaking and in the basics of how to organize thought and communicate a point within a limited time.

So why insert a chapter contrasting Toastmasters to a Keynote speech?

In brief, Toastmasters is an example of the typical formal speech training most receive whether in college, sales training programs, seminary, etc. It's good, but not necessarily strong for making true and lasting connections. It's technically helpful, but if our purpose is to lead and add value, it's not enough.

Philosophically, as I've shared earlier, most of the techniques taught in programs like Toastmaster's are designed to communicate with the head, not the heart per se. This isn't bad. But for keynotes, it's incomplete. Furthermore, I would add that it's incomplete for true connection, thus leadership communication.

Actually, there are several clear and distinct differences between keynote speaking and a public speaking club like Toastmasters. Here are just a few:

- The time. Keynotes vary, but range in length from 20-40 minutes. Club speeches run about 4-6 minutes.
- The expectation. People expect to be entertained in a keynote whereas club members want to be informed and/or to learn a new speaking technique by observation.
- The importance of content. A typical sales presentation or speech at Toastmaster's is 80% content. By content, I mean facts and information. In a good keynote, 20% is content and 80% is entertainment.
- The style/appearance. A good keynote speaker makes you think he's just "winging-it" and speaking "off the cuff." The truth is he's

practiced for hours and repeated every phrase hundreds of times. He seems to be responding to the audience and may even make mistakes (although those are often planned and rehearsed as well). Toastmaster's competitors present flawlessly with perfect diction, inflection, and gestures.

- The audience. A club audience is friendly whereas others may be downright hostile at times. A club audience, is tough in terms of content however, because they'll be watching and listening, NOT to learn something, but to find flaws in your style/approach. This won't typically be the focus of an outside business audience.
- The compensation. This is easy. Toastmaster's speakers present for free. Good keynoters may make $25-30,000 for a 25 minute speech.

- The follow-up. Keynote speakers are always looking for "the next step." That may be a workshop, coaching relationship, or a follow-up presentation. Thus, they ALWAYS have a program and an offer. Club speakers do not, nor should they.
- Body language and non-verbal signals. This is the subject of my next chapter. Suffice it to say here that keynote speakers send a more casual, relaxed signal to their audience.

One of my greatest examples of how the "chaos" of keynotes can lead to powerful connection was a message I gave recently. I don't even remember what I was talking about exactly, but I said, "Because…because…'Be-Cause, Be-Cause, Be-Cause, Be-Cause—Be Caaaaaaaaaaaaaaaaaaaauussse….," and of course they answered, "Because of the Wonderful Things He Does!" I was exaggerating the "because" statement for effect and the audience "ran with it." Everyone started laughing and then I said, "I don't even know where I was going" and one young guy in the audience shouted, "Follow the Yellow Brick Road!" That's when I really derailed the whole thing...before I thought about it, I shouted, "That's how you find the Urologist, not my train of thought."

Chaos ensued....one guy was laughing so hard, he literally almost fell off of his chair. I just walked away from the podium, put my head against the wall and said, "I'm sorry Lord...." It took me several minutes to regain control of the room...But it was worth it! We had connected! And for the rest of my presentation, they were right there with me! I would have failed a Toastmaster's contest—but I achieved the objective of communicating to connect! And by using some of the techniques in this book...so can you!

Chapter Nine: Body Language, Non-Verbal Signals, & Learning Styles

We now enter two other areas where the most common forms of formal speech, leadership, and communication training are lacking: the use of non-verbal techniques and the understanding of learning styles when presenting to an audience.

Let me start with a story that illustrates the powerful reality of non-verbal communication...

I remember visiting a woman who had attended my church regularly. She came alone because her husband had no interest and was in fact, quite hostile to the idea. He had served as a soldier in Hitler's army and was an angry, bitter man. Whenever I came into their home, he would growl from the next room and she'd have to tell him to "back off" so he'd quiet down and let us converse.

All this changed one day when he was diagnosed with terminal cancer and began to decline rapidly. In fact, he ended-up in the hospital on a respirator almost overnight. At her request, I went to see him in his room. I knew they had decided against maintaining life support and that the doctors would soon be "pulling the plug," so-to-speak. I knew this, she knew this…and so did my Nazi friend.

As soon as I came into the room, his tear-filled eyes met mine. He leaned forward, painfully pushing against the respirator tube in his throat and reached out for me with both hands. I drew close to the bedside and we had a powerful, yet unspoken conversation for several minutes. He couldn't utter a word, but I knew he was apologizing and seeking reconciliation not only with me, but with God.

I read somewhere that more than 90% of what people learn and remember comes from non-verbal communication. It's not what we say, but how we say it, how we look when saying it, the methods we use to say it, etc. Furthermore, since people forget 75% of what they hear within 48 hours, taking advantage of learning styles such as the kinesthetic so that people EXPERIENCE what we're communicating is Key!

All this being said, here are some tips for effective non-verbal communication:

- Smile! It's amazing how often we forget this simple little thing, but nothing will turn-off an audience more than a deadpan or frowning speaker. I love the old saying, "Smile, it makes people wonder what you're up to."

- Move around, but with purpose. There's a balance between standing rigidly behind the lectern and running all over the stage like the proverbial headless chicken. The best advice I've been given on this is to move naturally and with purpose. If I'm looking to my right, I might take two steps to my right and vise-versa. If I'm excited, my gestures will be bigger, etc. This keeps the audience focused.

- Lean in! If I speak quietly and lean toward you, you'll likely focus on me and lean toward me as well. This works to make a key point or regain control if the audience is drifting or becoming distracted.

- Mimic. You have to be careful with this one, but we tend to feel comfortable with people who look and act like us. So, if your audience is leaning back, you need to be laid back. If they are on the edge of their seats, you should lean into them. If people smile, smile back, etc. This works one-on-one as well as with large groups. You've got to be subtle about it though. If they think you're mocking them by playing "monkey see, monkey do," they'll reject you. Just try to occasionally mimic body language for that extra boost in connection.

- "Look at me when we're talking." As obvious as it seems, eye contact is critical. I remember a professor in college who used to stare over our heads into space. It didn't take long for us to join him—in space that is. Look into the "window of the soul" and you might be surprised what you find as you're attempting to communicate.

- Reach out and touch someone. This is another area where you have to be careful. Still, human touch is powerful. Just a quick hand on the shoulder or a quick "high-five" creates a connection and can go a long way toward having your message received.

- Gesture freely. I've heard so many opinions on this and frankly, they make me laugh. To follow verbatim, you'd look like a robot. My advice is simply, "be natural," when it comes to gestures. Don't exaggerate and don't feel self-consciously stiff. Just go with it. The key is to be relaxed and move as if you were talking to some close friends in your living room. If you can envision that, you'll do just fine.

- Don't cross your arms unless you *are* cross. The one gesture I wouldn't mimic whether one-on-one or in a group is to cross your arms. I realize some do it simply because they find it comfortable, but the universally-recognized signal it communicates is, "I'm not comfortable with you, I'm closed to what you're saying, and I want this to be <u>over</u>!" Avoid this one like the proverbial plague.

- Appeal to all styles unless you're communicating one-on-one. Remember that people take in information differently. We even favor one or more of our senses when experiencing something new. For example, if you took a group to the beach, some would describe the sound of the gulls and waves while others would talk about the feel of the sun and the sand on their skin. Some would describe the beautiful sky and the blue water, etc. On top of that, remember that there are multiple learning styles. Some learn kinesthetically by actively doing something. Others are auditory while others still are visual learners. If you're addressing a group, you need to appeal to all categories because they'll likely all be represented in the crowd.

- Read the non-verbal signals from your audience. If I see people talking or looking at their phones during a speech, I'll intentionally move in their direction in a friendly, non-threatening way just to recapture their attention. I might even joke with them or ask a question of that side of the room. If people look worried or happy, sad or afraid; I'm always measuring these non-verbal signals against what I'm communicating to make sure I'm connecting. If I tell a joke and someone looks angry or starts crying—I'm either not connecting or I'm communicating the wrong message. The only way I can fix this is to be sensitive enough to read it in the first place.

Developing these skills takes time. Still, the development process starts with a desire and a willingness to learn. Being sensitive to both verbal and non-verbal signals is critical, so choosing to develop in this area will pay dividends in your leadership and your ability to communicate.

Chapter Ten: One-on-One Communication, the Crown Jewel of Connection

Usually when I share this information in a workshop, I'll ask people to rate themselves with regard to settings. In other words, I'll ask them whether they feel more comfortable and effective when communicating one-on-one, in a small group, or with a large audience. It's amazing to me how often people choose one-on-one. Second is large groups. A distant third is almost always the small group setting.

Why?

Well, in many ways it comes down to lines of communication. In a one-on-one conversation, there are only two lines: one for each speaker. Add 2-3 more people and now each individual in the group is handling multiple lines both from himself to the group members and from those individuals back to him.

The reason this doesn't become MORE complicated in a large audience is that not everyone in the large audience is communicating back to the speaker. While there are many non-verbal ques (as we discussed in the last chapter), there are very few if any constant, verbal signals. In many ways therefore, a large audience acts like a single individual so there are still only two lines for the speaker to deal with: one going out from him to the audience, and one coming back from them as a collective "voice" to the speaker.

The bottom line is that the simplest form is the one-on-one setting and that's why it's so popular. The question is, how can we make it more effective and use it appropriately to influence and lead for good?

The first point I'll make here is that you have to actually choose to use it. I know that sounds silly, but you'd be amazed at how many leaders ignore and avoid one-on-one connections because it's too time consuming or just because they don't feel comfortable. The opportunity mentioned earlier to follow Stephen Covey's famous advice from his book, "Seven Habits of Highly Effective People," and thus "Seek first to understand…then to be understood," is incredible in this setting.

I would argue that it's ONLY when meeting one-on-one when we can truly begin to understand someone's basic motive/passion, their personality, their thought process/perception, etc. Avoiding individual connection with key staff members and leaders is a huge mistake.

The next key to making this work as a leader is to make the best choice as to when and how often to meet one-on-one. If you do it too often, it can become annoying and waste time. If not often enough, you'll lose the benefit of the ever-deepening connection possible. Make sure you do this enough to keep the connection flowing and growing and make sure you do it at times when you and your team member are both "at your best."

The last point regarding one-on-one connection and communication is to be sure of your role in this setting. I believe there are four primary people/positions every growing leader/team member needs to interact with: a coach, a mentor, a friend, and a boss. Let me describe each of these briefly:

Coach: Contrary to popular opinion, the coach is not the guy/gal who tells you what to do or not do. He/she isn't instructive or directive at all. No, a good coach asks the right questions and is an ever-curious, active listener who helps you understand your own inner voice. This enables you to reach your maximum potential by getting rid of the "stuff" in the way of progress and embracing the truth that's within you. If you're in this role, you ask questions and make almost no statements. You listen, and only speak for clarity, not to share information.

Mentor: A good mentor, on the other hand, gives lots of direction. He/she has "been there and done that" so he share his expertise and experience with the mentee. If you're in the mentoring role, you're expected to have answers and to share insights during your one-on-one meeting times.

Friend: Proverbs tells us that, "a friends loves at all time and a brother is born for adversity (Prov. 17:17)." Everyone needs people who just listen without judgment, instruction, or brainstorming. We all need friends who don't give advice without being asked and won't ask 100 questions every time we share something. Friends are peers who listen. This is important and very distinct from the other one-on-one communication roles.

Boss: We all know this one. This kind of individual communication comes from the guy "in charge." Similar to a mentor, a boss has an agenda. He/she may be in the role of mentor or even a coach at times, but the agenda is to accomplish certain tasks or fulfill a certain vision. This vision may or may not be what the individual wants, but no matter, it must be accomplished and that impacts the one-on-one connection in an obvious way.

Once you know your role, you've chosen to make one-on-one connections with key people, and you're clear on the logistics for making this happen, you're ready to make this mode of communication an integral part of your communication strategy.

Chapter Eleven: When to use email, letters, text messaging, or phones.

In this electronic, instant-communication age, it's ironic that nothing has done more damage to solid leadership communication than the misuse of texting and email for sensitive communication. One need look no further than the current Democratic primary race to see the potential turmoil circling Hilary Clinton and the question of using a private email server for classified communication.

But much less sensitive information can destroy a company or at least its culture when shared inappropriately. Even positive and encouraging messages can "miss the mark" when shared electronically instead of in person. There's just no human warmth in a text. Furthermore, it's impossible to see body language, hear tone of voice, or any other critical element of communication when reading it on a screen.

Sometimes, it's just more personal and healthy to talk face-to-face. I remember the days before Al Gore invented the internet (just kidding) when email was limited to local, mini-or-mainframe-based systems. Email was a new concept and everyone loved it. So, often, instead of talking to someone in the next cubicle, it was common for folks to just "zap them an email."

One day, after 4-5 different people in the same cubicle area had emailed me a note, I stood up so they could all see me (I'm about 6'5" tall) and shouted, "HEY—I'M RIGHT HERE! STOP SENDING ME EMAILS!"

So there's good and bad with all of this technology. With that in mind, let me share some "do's and don'ts" of electronic communication.

Do's

-Use text or email for quick reminders

-Electronically schedule routine meetings

-Send funny pictures of your dog

-Forward helpful posts or articles

Don'ts

-Reprimand someone electronically

-Debate pro's and cons of an idea

-Send anything you wouldn't want shared with millions

-Send funny/embarassing pictures of your boss

-Send political commentary unless that's your job.

I sometimes do impressions. I'm not "ready for prime time," but some of them are pretty good. For example, partly because I look like him, I do an excellent "John Maxwell." I used to do a very believable impression of one of my old Regional Vice Presidents when I sold in the technology sector. I could even call people as him to chew them out or make them squirm over a sales dispute, etc. It was fun, but cruel.

One day, I decided to email as my VP. I had learned to use certain phrases, etc., that he loved and it really came across as legit. Of course, everyone knew this was a joke since the email had my return info at the top. Still, I made our office manager laugh so hard, she cried while reading it.

Soon after my little email prank, the VP made an unexpected visit to our office. Later that day, during a meeting, he was introducing a new product idea when he turned to me and said, "Well, actually, maybe you should present this Joel. You seem to be doing a great job of BEING me lately!" Then, he read the email out loud.

You could have heard a pin drop in the room when he finished. He stared at me with a deadpan look and everyone, including me, thought my career there was over…until he threw his head back, and laughed hysterically. "Gotcha!" he exclaimed! I laughed nervously, knowing I had "dodged a bullet." Needless to say, I didn't send anymore impersonation emails!

I think you get the idea. The general principle is to use text, email, or even the phone when you have no other choice, but try to keep it to simple, basic, fact-based communication. Handle brain-storming, correction, debates, detailed training, vision-oriented conversations, etc., in person whenever possible.

Of course, the next best thing to in-person discussion would be to use an online meeting program so you can see each other and interact effectively. For example, in a recent leadership program I ran, we had one gentleman who joined our group weekly via Skype. It worked well, but, I would add that he had a pretty strong relationship with me and others in the group beforehand such that they were all intent on including him as what we called the "Max Headroom" contributor.

When you have no choice but to use the phone or some other online service to have a potentially sensitive conversation, here are a few suggestions. First, make sure you are understood before moving on to other topics/points. Repeat what you've heard the other person say and seek confirmation to be sure you've understood them as well. If you have a bad connection or static on the line, call back or perhaps even reschedule to make sure there's no misunderstanding or unnecessary hurt.

I think the key in all of this is to remember that human beings were created with innate social needs. We need to see and be seen, touch and be touched, hear and be heard, etc. The best way to do this is face-to-face. Still, electronic media can be helpful to share details and data. Keeping these things in mind can guide our choices and enhance our effectiveness greatly.

Chapter Twelve: Is Silence Golden? When Leaders Speak & When They're Quiet

I'm always amazed at how we assume that "silence is golden." It can be, but isn't always. How do you know when to remain silent?

- When someone else needs to speak and you need to hear them. We've dealt with this in earlier chapters, but one of the golden lessons of leadership is knowing when to listen or ask questions versus teaching, correcting, etc.

- When you need to think first. It's OK to take time to think unless you're facing an unavoidable deadline/crisis. Most often we're not, even if the think we are. It's appropriate to say, "I need a day to consider this," and mean it. That is, take a day, not months, consider, pray, and respond.

- When you need a "pregnant pause" for effect. Good keynote speakers do this all the time, but it works one-on-one too. I've fallen in love with the series, "Blue Bloods" on Netflix. The key figure, Commissioner Regan, played by Tom Selleck, uses these pauses masterfully in tense situations.

- When you need to "cool off" first. My lovely wife is a School Psychologist. I joke that she went into that field to learn how to cope with me. She's really good at what she does. One of her techniques is to teach kids how to "give yourself a time-out." Too bad adults don't do this more often. I can think of a couple presidential candidates who would benefit. Just take a break until the anger subsides enough for you to make a rational choice. It's simple really!

- When the other person needs the experience of "figuring it out." This is a hard one for me. I like to teach and share. If I see someone struggling to come-up with a good answer, I have to bite my tongue and put myself in an emotional straight jacket to avoid "filling in the silence" with a ton of great suggestions. Sometimes, this is more hurtful than helpful. Letting someone squirm and then come-up with the right answer is often best for their development.

Chapter Thirteen: When "Enough is enough!" How to Know Your Communication Worked!

As I sit to write this chapter, the first thing that comes to my mind is, "Duh!" In other words, it seems obvious that the primary way you'd know if your communication worked would be to watch the actions and the fruit as displayed in the lives of others. This is true, but it isn't a complete answer.

In order to look for and see fruit, you've got to know what the goal of your communication was to begin with. Did you want people to just know or understand something? Did you want them to do something or stop doing something? Was your goal to entertain, inform, or both?

The answers to these questions will determine how you measure success as a leader and communicator. Some things are clear and obvious—they either did it or they didn't do what you asked. Others are more subtle. It's the subtle, more difficult-to-measure objectives I'd like to address here.

Our education system has become obsessed with testing. Frankly, this is driven by the need for funding since funds won't continue if test scores are unsatisfactory. Still, many professionals in the field would argue that WHAT we're testing is insufficient as a measure of what kids are actually learning. This is even truer of adult audiences at workshops, meetings, etc., since:

    A. We don't typically test them formally.

B. We assume a certain level of comprehension that we wouldn't ascribe to children.

So how CAN you know that you're connecting and that there is comprehension when your goal was strictly to inform and/or entertain?

The first thing I look for is what Bill Gove, one who many refer to as the "Father of Modern Professional Speaking," called, "Payoffs." Every time an audience member or listener laughs, cries, nods, or makes a face; you've scored a payoff. In other words, it's a reaction demonstrating connection. The lack of a payoff doesn't always mean that you haven't made a connection, but seeing one is a measurable plus.

Next, I look for questions, complaints, and/or any type of feedback. If someone asks me a question or says something afterwards that indicates thought—I've won. There's a connection! Again, we can't argue the opposite using an argument from silence. Still, these direct conversations indicate that we've gotten through to the listener.

Another measure is to use feedback forms or formal questioning. A good feedback form is like a pop quiz in school. Teachers know whether or not little Johnny was listening based on his score when given a quick quiz afterwards. Feedback forms not only tell you whether or not a listener liked your presentation, if worded correctly, they can tell you whether or not they understood or got something from it. Finally, a good feedback form allows for contact via email or phone, etc., to provide more information at a later date (see appendix for a sample).

So, we've talked about measuring results even when you present to strangers. Still, we'd all agree that the best and most effective presentations/conversations occur when there's an ongoing relationship with your listeners versus a "one and done" scenario. You'll experience the best and most measurable results when communicating to lead a group which will be with you for an extended period of time. Our next chapter deals with leading via communication, the ultimate conclusion of this book….

Chapter Fourteen: Leadership Communication—Adding Value through Influence & Connection

The Bible speaks of the tongue as a rudder that steers even the biggest of ships (James 3:1-12). Like it or not, what you say and how you say it will set the course for your organization on a regular basis. The first step in good leadership communication practice is to embrace this fact! Ignore it, and it will destroy you. Use it, and it will bring blessings.

The good news of our modern age is that technology has made communication instantaneous. And the bad news is, technology has made communication instantaneous. If you do it well, it pays dividends. If not, the pain and loss happen at light speed.

The goal of this book has been to help you use communication to lead, that is, to influence for positive change in the lives of others. As a speaker, trainer, and author, that's always my focus as well, so I invite you to continue this journey with us in one of the following ways:

- Attend one of our half or full day seminars. You can find out more about these and even purchase recorded versions online at www.communicatetolead.com.

- Read our other books and resources available on our website, at retailers like www.amazon.com, or by calling 860-938-2725.

- Invite me to do a keynote address at your next meeting. We've included a list of primary topics and workshop subjects in our appendix as well.

- Call to schedule a free coaching consult and consider a long-term coaching relationship. Some communication strategies are more complex and take time to implement. If this is your situation, please feel free to call us at 860-938-2725.

- Participate in a Mastermind group based on this book or John Maxwell's, "Everyone Communicates, Few Connect." These groups, often done by conference call, are application and peer-support oriented. We take 8-12 leaders and work through questions based on each chapter of the book in question. The goal is to apply the principles in your context and help others in the group do the same.

Whatever your context and specific need, we truly wish you great success as you continue to communicate to lead and thus enhance the lives of those around you!

Appendix:

Footnotes

1. Maxwell, John C, *The 21 Irrefutable Laws of Leadership,* Nashville, TN, Thomas Nelson, 2007.

2. "Top 50 Leadership and Management Experts". Inc. Magazine. Retrieved May 10, 2014.

3. www.ziglar.com/quotes.

4. Maxwell, John C., *Good Leaders Ask Great Questions,* New York, NY, Hachette Book Group, 2014.

5. Maxwell, John C. & Dornan, Jim *Becoming a Person of Influence,* Nashville, TN, Thomas Nelson, 1997.

6. Rissinger, Joel L., *Whole 4 Life,* Newington, CT, Communicate to Lead Publishing, 2015.

7. Ibid., Pages 13-22.

8. Coven, Stephen R., *7 Habits of Highly Effective People,* New York, NY, Simon & Schuster, November, 2013.

9. Rissinger, Joel L., *The Crucified Couple,* Newington, CT, *Communicate to Lead Publishing,* 2014, Pages 57-63.

10. Maxwell, John C., *Good Leaders Ask Great Questions,* New York, NY, Hachette Book Group, 2014.

About the Author

Pastor Joel L. Rissinger is the President of Communicate to Lead, a certified speaker and coach with the John Maxwell Group, and the Lead and Founding Pastor of Mill Pond Church in Newington, Connecticut. More importantly, he has been married to Karen Rissinger, for more than 31 years. Together, they have two adult children, an awesome son-in-law, and a beautiful granddaughter, Aadi Joy Elise. Pastor Joel started his career as a Management Consultant to companies like Johnson & Johnson, Eastman Kodak, and Saft Battery where he did personality assessment, motivational assessment, outplacement counseling, and recruiting. He also served for several years as a Marketing Executive, consulting and providing information technology solutions to companies like Bell Aerospace, Xerox, Kodak, Marriott Corporation, the State of CT, and Welch Foods.

Since 1992, Pastor Joel has been in vocational ministry, but has kept his hand in business as well. Joel has been ordained by Converge USA, as well as two other organizations. In this capacity, he has led several congregations through major transitions prior to planting Mill Pond Church in 2007. In addition, Joel has served as the Director of Church Multiplication for Converge Northeast, the New England Regional Coordinator for The Antioch School of Leadership Development, Seminar Presenter for Life Innovations, Inc., and as a Chaplain for several local companies. Pastor Joel has been a regular speaker at the Northeast Regional Iron Sharpens Iron Conferences, the Liberty University Church Planting Emphasis Week, the Newington, CT Chamber of Commerce meetings, numerous Rotary Clubs, the CT Better Business Bureau, and other venues. In addition to his John Maxwell Team certification, Joel is a graduate of the Bill Gove Speech Workshop. He has a BA in theology from Ambassador University, and MAs in both religion and religious education from Liberty University. He is the author of several books including *The Crucified Church, The Crucified Couple, and Whole 4 Life.*

Leadership Seminar Topics by Joel L. Rissinger

1. **"Speak to the Heart...Or, Talk to the Hand!"** This seminar focuses on communicating to connect and lead/influence others for good. We deal with principles and techniques to connect with the mind and the hearts/emotions of those we care about. It's loosely based on John Maxwell's book, "Everyone Communicates...Few Connect," as well as my new book, "Communicate to Lead." This is also available as a keynote speech—see short example at www.communicatetolead.com.

2. **"Living Intentionally."** Loosely based on John Maxwell's book, this session talks about how we should lead by taking initiative to serve and make a difference with our spouses, families, at work, and in the community. Leaders don't live by accident, they lead/influence "on purpose." This seminar talks about doing this well in a team environment.

3. **"What is true leadership?"** This is a compilation of 4-5 primary lessons learned through my certification as a John Maxwell Team speaker and coach. In it, I share John's view of what leadership is, how one grows as a leader, how we reproduce leadership in the lives of others, etc.

4. **"Leadership Gold."** This full or half-day JMT workshop is based on some the most powerful lessons learned by the #1 Leadership Expert in the World, John Maxwell. It can also be introduced as a kenonte where we share some of the pimary lessons in a 30 minute format.

5. **"Put Your Dream to the Test."** Everyone has dreams for their professional and personal life. Most people don't attain theirs and that's because, in part, they haven't clarified, tested, planned for, and consistently pursued their dreams. This workshop, based on John Maxwell's book by the same title, challenges teams to work together to establish and pursue a vision that will be attainable.

6. **"Becoming a Person of Influence."** John Maxwell defines leadership as "influence." I add that its influence that leads to measurable positive change. All of us have influence and, as we increase that influence, we accomplish more and find fulfillment. This workshop is great for managers, sales people, and executives who want to increase their ability to lead/influence others for good.

7. **"15 Invaluable Laws of Growth."** People want to grow. Companies want to grow. Churches want to grow. This workshop presents John Maxwell's wisdom and experience in teaching millions of people and hundreds of companies grow and attain success.

8. **"How to be a REAL Success."** Who doesn't want to be successful? In this presentation (also available as a workshop) we present four keys to true success—things many seminars neglect to teach. Based on John's best-selling book by the same title, this material can help you attain success or refine and clarify your success as you reach you goals.

The F.A.S.T. Track to find and equip new leaders:

Surveys indicate that the biggest challenge faced by leaders is developing new leaders. How do you continue to do your job, especially in a small company or church congregation and find time to build up new leaders? Still, this is critical to success both now and for the future of your organization.

To assist, we've developed the F.A.S.T. Track. I'll break it down briefly here, but understand that we offer this in more depth during several of our workshops:

F-ind them! No kidding! You already knew that was hard, but what I encourage clients to do is to look for leaders in unexpected places. Often, we want the most compliant, submissive, quiet and obedient people as our underlings. Truth is, those aren't normally your leaders. The leaders are the ones rocking the boat. Many leadership development challenges exist because we're, like the old song, "Lookin' for (leaders) in all the wrong places!"

A-ssess them! We use several tools in this regard, but Mels Carbonnell's "Uniquely You" is the best in my estimation. Go to www.uniquelyyou.com for more information. You'll also find helpful tools for assessing motivation, passion, etc. in my book, "Whole 4 Life." The bottom line is that you need to know what makes your future leaders "tick" so you can lead and develop them appropriately.

S-chool them! I believe in a very simple model. Of course you need to give them leadership instruction. We do this and are happy to help. Beyond that though, "hands-on" mentoring is the most effective method. You tell them what to do, you let them watch you do it, you go with them to watch them do it, and then you turn them loose. In my experience, it's the last part that's the hardest. Most leaders are scared to let new leaders "fly solo" and maybe make mistakes. This is absolutely necessary though and is a "safe bet" if the other steps have been followed first.

T-utor them for life! Just because you've turned over the reins to a new leader doesn't mean you've cut them out of your life and ceased to be a help for them. Frankly, just the opposite. You should ALWAYS be available for them to ask questions or just be a sounding board for new ideas. This also helps you feel more comfortable when you do "turn them loose" because you know it's not the end of the relationship.

Five Minute Personality Test
Lion – Otter – Golden Retriever – Beaver

Choose the items in each line that is most like you and put a 4. Then pick the item that is next most like you and put a 3. Then a 2 and then 1 which is least like you. Do this across the page for each list of descriptors.

1. ___ Likes authority	___ Enthusiastic	___ Sensitive Feelings	___ Likes Instruction
2. ___ Takes Charge	___ Takes Risks	___ Loyal	___ Accurate
3. ___ Determined	___ Visionary	___ Calm	___ Consistent
4. ___ Enterprising	___ Verbal	___ Enjoys Routine	___ Predictable
5. ___ Competitive	___ Promoter	___ Dislikes Change	___ Practical
6. ___ Problem Solver	___ Enjoys Popularity	___ Gives in To Others	___ Factual
7. ___ Productive	___ Fun-loving	___ Avoids Confrontations	___ Responsible
8. ___ Bold	___ Likes Variety	___ Sensitive	___ Prefers Perfection
9. ___ Decision Maker	___ Spontaneous	___ Nurturing	___ Detail Oriented
10. ___ Persistent	___ Inspirational	___ Peace Maker	___ Analytical

Total: ___

Lion — This personality likes to lead. The lion is good at making decisions and is very goal-oriented. They enjoy challenges, difficult assignments, and opportunity for advancement. Because lions are thinking of the goal, they can step on people to reach it. Lions can be very aggressive and competitive. Lions must learn not to be too bossy or to take charge in other's affairs.

Strength: Goal-oriented, strong, direct
Weakness: Argumentative, too dictatorial
Limitation: Doesn't understand that directness can hurt others, hard time expressing grace.

Otter — Otters are very social creatures. Otter personalities love people. They enjoy being popular and influencing and motivating others. Otters can sometime be hurt when people do not like them. Otter personalities usually have lots of friends, but not deep relationships. They love to goof-off. (They are notorious for messy rooms.) Otters like to hurry and finish jobs. (Jobs are not often done well.) The otter personality is like Tigger in Winnie The Pooh.

Strength: People person, open, positive
Weakness: Talks too much, too permissive
Limitation: Remembering past commitments, follow through with discipline

Golden Retriever — Good at making friends. Very loyal. Retriever personalities do not like big changes. They look for security. Can be very sensitive. Very caring. Has deep relationships, but usually only a couple of close friends. Wants to be loved by everyone. Looks for appreciation. Works best in a limited situation with a steady work pattern.

Strength: Accommodating, calm, affirming
Weakness: Indecisive, indifferent, unable to express emotional, too soft on other people
Limitation: Seeing the need to be more assertive, holding others accountable.

Beaver — Organized. Beavers think that there is a right way to do everything and they want to do it exactly that way. Beaver personalities are very creative. They desire to solve everything. Desire to take their time and do it right. Beavers do not like sudden changes. They need reassurance.

Strength: High standards, order, respect
Weakness: Unrealistic expectations of self & others, too perfect.
Limitation: Seeing the optimistic side of things, expressing flexibility

The JOHN MAXWELL Team

AN INDEPENDENT CERTIFIED COACH, TEACHER AND SPEAKER
WITH THE JOHN MAXWELL TEAM

FEEDBACK FORM

Thank you so much for attending my presentation today. My goal is to add value to you, your business/non-profit enterprise, and to those you impact! Please take a minute to fill-out this form to help me prepare for further service.

1. Expectations. Did today's session meet or exceed your expectations? Why or why not?
....
....
....

2. Take-Away. What did you find most helpful and thus is your primary "take-away" from this message?
....
....
....

3. Improvements. What would you like to see as a change to this presentation. Any additions or deletions suggested?
....
....
....

4. Follow-up. Please choose at least one of the following:

( ) Yes. I'd like more information on leadership development.
( ) Yes. I'd like more information about holding a leadership development workshop at my church.
( ) Yes. I'd like to have Pastor Joel contact me about doing a couples enrichment session with my spouse.
( ) Yes. I'd like more information about one-on-one coaching with Pastor Joel
( ) Yes. I'd like to participate in a leadership "Mastermind Group" with Pastor Joel
( ) Yes. I'd like more information on having Pastor Joel share a workshop at my church.
( ) I'm all set for now, but would like to receive emails on upcoming seminars, etc.
( ) I am taking advantage of the special offer from this session. Please circle: AM Session   PM Session

5. Contact Info:
Name: _____
Church: _____
Email: _____
Cell: _____

** Thank you for taking the time to complete this important document. Please hand it to a Joel Rissinger Team member before you leave.

Made in the USA
Middletown, DE
10 May 2016